W9-CBM-894

Women Inventors

1

*Margaret Knight, Cynthia Westover,
Elizabeth Hazen and Rachel Brown,
Ruth Handler*

by Jean F. Blashfield

Capstone Press

MINNEAPOLIS

Copyright © 1996 Capstone Press. All rights reserved. No part of this book may be reproduced in any form without written permission from the publisher.

Printed in the United States of America.

Capstone Press • 2440 Fernbrook Lane • Minneapolis, MN 55447

Editorial Director   John Coughlan
Managing Editor   Tom Streissguth
Production Editor   James Stapleton
Book Design   Timothy Halldin
Picture Researcher   Athena Angelos

Library of Congress Cataloging-in-Publication Data

Blashfield, Jean F.
    Women inventors / by Jean F. Blashfield.
        p.   cm. -- (Capstone short biographies)
    Includes bibliographical references and index.
    Summary: Each volume presents brief accounts of five women and their inventions.
    ISBN 1-56065-274-8
    1. Women inventors--United States--Biography--Juvenile literature. 2. Inventions--United States--History--Juvenile literature. [1. Inventors. 2. Inventions. 3. Women--Biography.] I. Title. II. Series.
    T39.B53   1996
    609.2'273--dc20   95-442
    [B]   CIP
                                                                          AC

Table of Contents

Ruth Handler 5

Margaret Knight 13

Cynthia Westover 18

Elizabeth Hazen and Rachel Brown 26

More about Inventing 34

Glossary 38

To Learn More 40

Places to Visit 43

Some Useful Addresses 45

Index 47

Ruth Handler
1916-
Filling a Need

Ruth Handler is a woman who recognizes a need and does something about it. When her daughter, Barbie, was a child in the 1940s, Mrs. Handler sometimes watched her play with paper dolls. The flat, cardboard dolls had big wardrobes. Barbie would dress and undress them and design more clothes for them.

Mrs. Handler knew that her daughter would rather be playing with a doll that was more realistic than a flat paper one. But there was no doll on the market that had a figure like a grown-up. Instead, most dolls were round and pudgy and babyish.

Barbie Handler's way of playing with dolls stayed in her mother's mind.

The Toy Company

Ruth Handler was born in Denver, Colorado, in 1916. She married her high school boyfriend, Elliot Handler, and lived with him in Los Angeles, California. They had two children, Barbie and Ken.

All dolls used to look like babies. Ruth Handler knew that many girls wanted a doll that seemed more adult.

The Handlers had a furniture-making business. The furniture makers often built doll house furniture with leftover scrap wood. In 1946, the Handlers started a toy company, the Mattel Company, to sell the toy furniture. Mattel eventually became the largest toy company in the world. One of the reasons it grew was Ruth Handler's doll.

Ruth Handler saw that girls like her daughter, Barbie, wanted a new kind of doll, a teenage doll with an adult figure. She sketched a beautiful doll with a slender waist, pretty hair, long legs, and joints that could be moved.

Ruth asked an artist to make and remake the figure until it was just right. Someone else created ways for the doll's hips, arms, and neck to bend. The doll was named Barbie, after Ruth's daughter. The people who helped Ruth create the doll also have their names on the doll's **patents**.

Barbie's many different outifts allow girls to dress her up for different occasions.

Popular Barbie

Barbie Doll was first sold in 1959. Mattel's advertising said, "Girls of all ages will thrill to the fascination of her miniature wardrobe of fine-fabric fashions: tiny zippers that really zip . . . coats with luxurious linings . . . jeweled earrings and necklaces . . . and every girl can be the star."

There had never been a doll like Barbie. She was an instant hit with girls everywhere and has remained so ever since. Several years after Barbie made her appearance in toy stores, she got a boyfriend, Ken, named after Ruth Handler's other child. She also has a sister, Skipper, and two friends, Midge and Christie, an African American.

Barbie and her friends are now found all over the world. Some Barbie Dolls are sold in

Ken was named after Ruth Handler's own son.

special costumes. They wear the clothes of many nations, just like the girls who play with them.

Helping Women

In 1970, Ruth Handler was told that she had breast cancer. The serious, frightening illness inspired her to invent again.

The only way to treat breast cancer at that time was to remove the breast. The operation can make a woman feel a great loss, both physically and emotionally. Ruth tried to find an artificial breast that was both attractive and comfortable. She didn't like any of those she found.

Ruth put together a team of engineers and designers to create better artificial breasts. The designers did not just draw their ideas. They talked to and measured real women all over the country.

Finally, Ruth patented the artificial breasts under the name Nearly Me. They are made of a foam base covered by small compartments containing a thick liquid chemical called silicone. They feel and move as if they were real. Right breasts are different from left breasts. Like real breasts, Nearly Me artificial breasts come in many different sizes. Ruth Handler started a new company, called Ruthton, to make and sell the artificial breasts.

Today, many women, who as little girls thanked Ruth Handler for her Barbie Doll, thank the same woman for the artificial breasts she invented. She has helped them live a normal life again after cancer surgery.

There are now dozens of different Barbie Dolls sold all over the world.

Margaret E. Knight

Bag Machine

Fig. 3

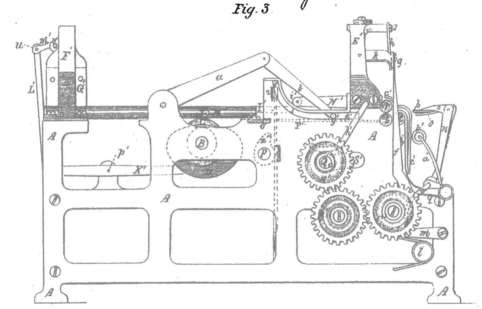

Fig. 4

Fig 5

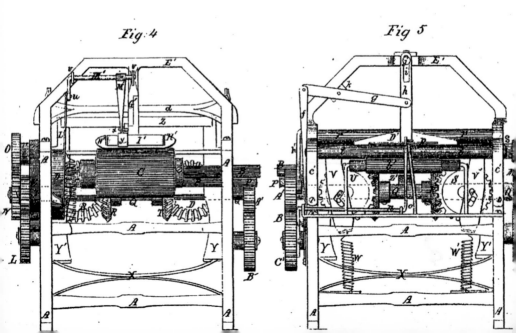

Margaret Knight
1838-1914
Fighting to Get Her Patent

Her mind was busy as she studied the machines in the room where she was working. It was 1868. Mattie Knight had just gone to work for a company that made paper bags.

Mattie was fascinated by machines. Even though she had little education, she had an understanding of how machines worked.

Mattie wondered if she could make a machine that would fold and glue a flat bottom into a paper bag. Paper bags had been in use for a long time. But in those days they were flat, like envelopes. Bags of that shape are not

This patent drawing for Margaret Knight's bag machine shows all of its moving parts.

very useful for bulky objects. Flat-bottomed bags had to be made by hand.

Mattie started experimenting at home. After two years of working day and night, she made a working model of a machine out of wood. With it, she made hundreds of perfect flat-bottomed bags. But she knew the machine would have to be made of iron if she was going to get a patent.

The Young Mattie

Margaret E. Knight had been making things all her life. Born in York, Maine, in 1838, Mattie was interested in how things worked even as a child. She was happier making toys for her brothers than playing with toys herself. Her brothers called her a tomboy, but she did not let the teasing bother her.

At 12, Mattie was living in Manchester, New Hampshire. She and her brothers worked in a textile mill there. She was horrified when she saw a man injured by a metal-tipped shuttle that fell out of a weaving machine. Mattie immediately thought of a way to stop the machine automatically when a shuttle fell out. The mill probably used her invention, but we don't know for sure.

Mattie worked at many different jobs and learned many different skills. Most of the jobs were things women did not do at that time, like photography, carpentry, and upholstery.

The Patent in Court

Mattie Knight never thought about patenting anything until she invented the paper-bag folding machine. An iron worker copied Mattie's wooden machine in iron. Taking it to Boston, Mattie asked another iron worker to make improvements on it before she sent the model to the U.S. Patent Office.

A man named Charles Annan saw the iron model and quickly copied it. Annan sent his copy of the bag-making machine to the Patent Office and claimed that he had invented it. Mattie hired a lawyer to help her prove that the bag maker was actually hers. She gathered up records, models, and the testimony of witnesses and sent them to Washington, D.C.

In 1871, after studying everything Mattie sent, the judge said that, yes, indeed, the clever bag machine must be Miss Knight's invention. But he added a statement that her success was "a matter of great surprise." That did not please Mattie at all. But she was granted a patent, her first, on the machine.

Mattie was offered a lot of money to sell the patent, but she chose not to. She was as smart at business matters as she was at figuring out machinery. She found a partner to start a company to produce the bag-making machines. Soon she patented two more inventions that made her paper bags even better.

Lady Edison

Mattie Knight took the money from her bag-making inventions and set up a laboratory and workshop in Boston. There she worked on whatever caught her attention. She created machines to cut the soles of shoes. She made an improvement on the mechanism that makes windows open and close. She also designed a rotary engine used to provide power in factories.

Over the years, Mattie Knight was granted at least 22 patents. After her death, Margaret Knight's picture hung on the wall of the U.S. Patent Office in Washington, D.C. Called Lady Edison, after the noted inventor Thomas Edison, Mattie was the most famous woman inventor of the time.

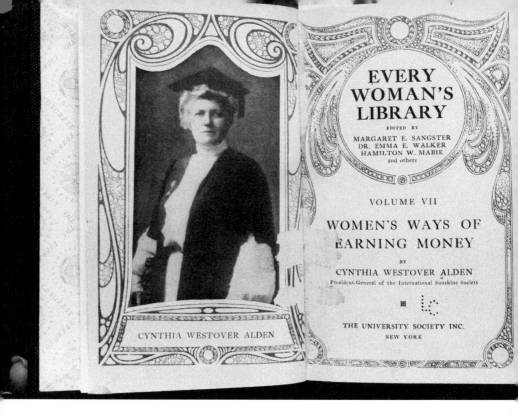

CYNTHIA WESTOVER ALDEN

EVERY
WOMAN'S
LIBRARY

EDITED BY

MARGARET E. SANGSTER
DR. EMMA E. WALKER
HAMILTON W. MABIE
and others

VOLUME VII

WOMEN'S WAYS OF
EARNING MONEY

BY

CYNTHIA WESTOVER ALDEN

President-General of the International Sunshine Society

THE UNIVERSITY SOCIETY INC.
NEW YORK

Cynthia Westover
?1858-1931
The Woman of Many Careers

At the end of the 19th century, the streets
of New York City were filthy. The horses that
pulled buggies and streetcars soiled the streets.
People threw trash and garbage from their
houses.

The work of cleaning the streets was done mainly by men and women with brooms. The piles of trash they swept up often blew away before they could be hauled away. They then had to be swept up again.

Horses pulled heavy loads of trash up ramps and dumped it into boats. The boats took the trash out into the harbor. The horses that pulled the loads often did not live very long.

Cynthia Westover, who worked for the New York City Streets Commission, knew that the method did not work well. Also, she felt sorry for the horses.

Before Westover invented the dumping cart, horses had to drag heavy trash wagons through the streets.

A sweeper uses his trash cart in the New York streets.

Westover set about designing a cart that the street cleaners could push. Without waiting for a wagon, they could deposit the swept-up piles of trash into the cart. The cart also had a derrick, or crane, that would lift the heavy load of trash right into the boats.

Raised to be Independent

Cynthia May Westover was born in Colorado, probably in 1858. Her father was a prospector for valuable minerals. Her mother had died when Cynthia was a baby.

Cynthia's father took her traveling with him into the mountains. He taught Cynthia, whom he called Bushy, that she could do whatever she set her mind to. She became an expert shot. She was killing buffalo before she was a teen-ager. She also learned mathematics and music.

While still a teenager, Bushy became a supervisor, or leader, in a factory. That job earned her enough money to attend Colorado State University. After receiving a diploma in 1882, independent young Cynthia headed for New York City.

In New York, Cynthia studied and taught both music and geology. In order to get a job, she passed the exam that people had to take before going to work for the government.

Helping the Cities

Cynthia became a customs inspector, working with people who arrived from other countries. Her job was to make sure they were not bringing into the United States things they

As a customs inspector, Westover examined immigrants as they arrived in New York.

should not. In this job, she became well known for her ability to speak many languages.

When another customs official was put in charge of the streets of New York City, he asked Westover to become his private secretary. It was in this job that she worked on her only invention. In 1892, Cynthia Westover received a patent for a "dumping cart with movable body and self-emptying derrick."

Westover's dumping cart won a gold medal from the French Academy of Inventors. That meant that her cart was the world's most clever invention of the year. Soon it was being sold to cities all over the world. She did not earn any money from the invention because she invented the cart while she was employed by New York City. The rights to the patent belonged to her employer.

Encouraging Independence

Soon after her invention was patented, Cynthia married a newspaper reporter named John Alden. She started to write newspaper articles and she illustrated them with her own photographs.

Many of her articles encouraged women to prepare themselves to earn their own living. She wrote, "every woman not an invalid can earn her own living if she really wants to do so." She thought that women should not have to depend on their husbands and fathers to earn their living. She wrote a book, *Women's Ways of Earning Money*, that gave them ideas on how to go about it.

Although Cynthia and her husband had no children of their own, she was very interested in children. She started an organization to help blind children. She also wrote books for girls, which included stories about Bushy and her adventures in the Rocky Mountains. Bushy,

The bin of Westover's new dumping cart could be lifted, and its contents placed in a waiting boat.

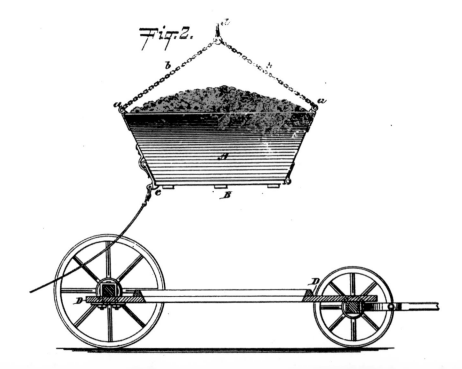

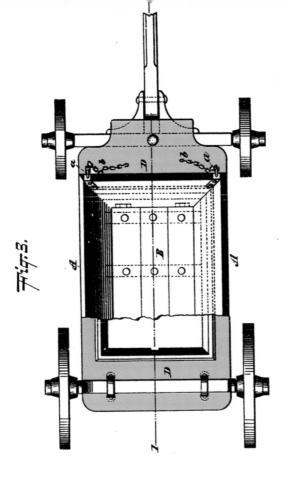

Fig. 3.

who encouraged girls to be independent, became a very popular character.

Cynthia Westover Alden was sure that women could do whatever they wanted to do. She showed by her own careers and her invention that this was so.

Elizabeth Hazen
1885-1975
Rachel Brown
1898-1980
Fungus Fighters

Surrounding Dr. Elizabeth Hazen in her
laboratory were jars containing samples of soil
from all over the world. Taking one sample at
a time, she mixed a little soil with some salt
water. Then she smeared the liquid on a
jellylike substance in a low, flat saucer.

Day by day, she studied the material in the
saucers. Some days she found something
growing in them. Other times nothing
happened. The jelly was a nutrient, or food, on
which very tiny plants or animals, called
microorganisms, could feed and grow. When
the microorganisms grew, they could be seen
and identified.

Making such tiny living things grow on a
nutrient is called culturing. Dr. Hazen had

Hazen and Brown worked together to develop useful disease-fighting antibiotics.

grown many **cultures** during her career in the laboratory of the New York State Department of Health. She grew these cultures to help doctors identify diseases their patients had.

But in these soil samples she was looking for something else. She was looking for a way to cure diseases.

Searching for Antibiotics

During World War II, doctors learned about **penicillin**, the first drug that could stop deadly **infections**. Many wounded soldiers who might have died without penicillin survived and came home.

Penicillin was the first **antibiotic**. Penicillin and other antibiotics kill harmful living microorganisms called **bacteria**. But there are other living things that cause diseases. Some, called **fungi**, cannot be killed by the same antibiotics used against bacteria.

A fungus is one of a big group of plants that are not green. Big fungi include mushrooms. Microscopic fungi are everywhere in the air, in soil, in water, and in our bodies.

Ringworm and the foot itch called athlete's foot are examples of skin diseases caused by fungi. Other kinds of fungi cause diseases with symptoms similar to the flu or the lung disease called pneumonia.

Dr. Elizabeth Hazen was looking for an antibiotic to treat fungus diseases.

Fascinated by Science

Elizabeth Lee Hazen was born in Mississippi in 1885. Her parents died when she was very young. Raised by her relatives, she worked hard to earn money to attend college. After getting her college degree, she taught high school science for many years while she kept going to school. She was 42 years old before she earned her Ph.D., the highest possible college degree, in bacteriology, the study of bacteria.

In 1931, Dr. Hazen went to work for the state health department in New York City. The scientists in her department were studying the bacteria-caused diseases people were suffering. Hazen learned all she could about fungus diseases as well. Gradually she built up a collection of cultures that has helped many people understand fungus diseases.

During her research, Dr. Hazen heard about Dr. Rachel Brown, a scientist who had discovered soil bacteria that produced an important antibiotic called streptomycin.

Streptomycin almost wiped out a terrible lung disease, tuberculosis. Hazen decided to investigate other soil bacteria, hoping to find one that would fight fungal diseases. Dr. Brown was soon working with her.

Dr. Brown Joins In

Rachel Brown was born in Massachusetts in 1898. Her father left the family when she was 14. Rachel's mother took care of two children and her own parents by herself.

A friend of her grandmother's paid Rachel's way to college. While she was a college student, Rachel discovered that she liked chemistry. After earning a Ph.D. in chemistry, she went to work at a New York state laboratory.

Dr. Hazen and Dr. Brown began to work together in 1948. Dr. Hazen continued to live and work in New York City. Dr. Brown worked in Albany, 150 miles (240 kilometers) away. They shared their work, including many cultures in glass tubes, by mail. Dr. Hazen made cultures of soil samples from all over the world. When she found a culture that seemed to stop the growth of a fungus, she mailed it to Dr. Brown in Albany. Dr. Brown would try to find out just what substance in the culture acted against the fungus. When she separated out the substance, she sent it back to Dr. Hazen to test again.

Dr. Hazen made the useful substances weaker and weaker to see how little could be used to fight a fungus disease. When the

substances poisoned mice, they knew they could not use them on humans. The women kept hunting.

The Wonder Drug

After many months, the two women found one substance that worked best. It came from microorganisms in soil that Dr. Hazen had dug up in Virginia. They made the substance purer and purer. They knew they were on to something important when it killed many different fungi but did not harm mice.

In 1950, Dr. Hazen and Dr. Brown announced their discovery. They called it **nystatin**, after New York State. They applied for a patent to protect their discovery from being copied. Without that patent application to protect the discovery, no drug company would have wanted to do the work of turning a little laboratory sample into a usable drug.

A drug company eventually spent four years and a lot of money testing and producing nystatin. Finally, the discovery of Dr. Hazen and Dr. Brown was being sold as tablets in

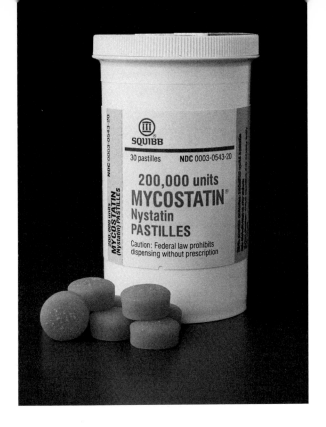

drugstores under the name Mycostatin. The patent covering the invention was not granted until 1957, seven years after the women made their application.

By then, people all over the world were recovering from serious illnesses because of the wonder drug. In 1975, Drs. Hazen and Brown became the first women to receive the important Chemical Pioneer Award.

More about Inventing

A patent is a government ruling that a certain person invented a new product or improved an old product. When a patent is granted, no one else can copy that new item, method, or design.

One of the first laws passed by the new United States of America, in 1790, was a patent law. The right of people to protect their inventions is also granted in the U.S. Constitution.

A patent keeps other people from copying an idea. But the period of the patent is not always the same. A new process or device or a new kind of plant is patented for 17 years. A design for the appearance of a product can be patented for only 14 years.

A Young Inventor

One of the youngest inventors ever to receive an American patent was Jeanie Low of Houston, Texas. On March 10, 1992, when she was 10 years old, she received a patent for her Kiddie Stool.

The Kiddie Stool is a child's stool mounted on a bathroom cabinet door. A child can pull the stool down and stand on it to wash her hands. The stool is held up by magnets on the door until the child is ready to use it. Jeanie's inventive mind started working on the problem when her own stool, made of plastic, broke when it caught in a door.

What to Do With a Good Idea

You may have a bright idea for a new or improved product. You need to know how it can be produced. You also have to figure out what claims you can make for it. Are all of its

NO MODEL.

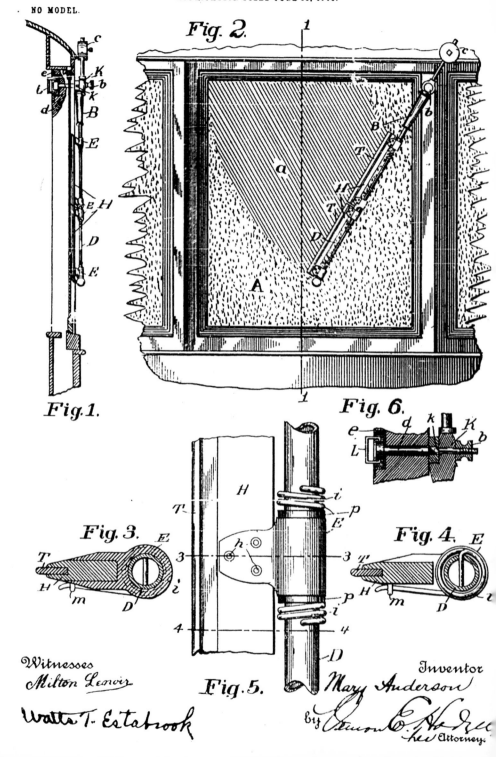

Fig. 2.

Fig. 1.

Fig. 6.

Fig. 3.

Fig. 5.

Fig. 4.

Witnesses
Milton Lenoir

Watts T. Estabrook

Inventor
Mary Anderson

by Cannon C. Hodge
her Attorney.

parts new? What is it good for? Just how useful is it?

Many people have a lawyer help them find out whether anything about their invention is already protected by another patent. The lawyer can help an inventor file the right papers for a patent. For more information on the details of obtaining a patent, write:

Office of Information
U.S. Patent Office
Washington, D.C. 20231

or:

Canadian Intellectual Property Office
Industry Canada
Place du Portage, Phase I
50 Victoria Street
Hull, Québec K1A 0C9
Canada

Glossary

antibiotic–a drug that keeps harmful microorganisms from growing and making people sick

bacteria–microscopic single-celled living things (neither plant nor animal) found everywhere. Some are helpful, some are harmful.

culture–a test in which a microorganism is grown on a nutrient, or food, substance in order to identify it

fungi–plants that do not contain green coloring material. Many are microscopic and live in soil. Some cause diseases.

infection–a disease caused by a microorganism invading the body

microorganism–a living plant or animal so small that it can be seen only with a microscope

newfangled–newly made and novel

nystatin–the first antibiotic against fungi, discovered and patented by Drs. Hazen and Brown. The antibiotic was named after New York State.

patent–a ruling by the government that a device or an improvement in a device was created by a certain person

penicillin–the first antibiotic against bacteria, discovered in 1928 by Alexander Fleming but not used until World War II

To Learn More

Aaseng, Nathan. *Twentieth-Century Inventors.*
New York: Facts on File, 1991.

Bundles, A'Lelia Perry. *Madam C.J. Walker.*
New York: Chelsea House Publishers, 1991.

Epstein, Vivian Sheldon. *History of Women in
Science for Young People.* Denver, Colo.:
VSE Publishers, 1994.

James, Portia P. *The Real McCoy: African-
American Invention and Innovation, 1619-
1930.* Washington, D.C.: Smithsonian
Institution, 1989.

Lafferty, Peter. *The Inventor Through History.*
New York: Thompson Learning, 1993.

Macaulay, David. *The Way Things Work.*
Boston: Houghton Mifflin, 1988.

McKissack, Patricia and McKissack, Fredrick. *African-American Inventors.* Brookfield, Conn.: The Millbrook Press, 1994.

Pizer, Vernon. *Shortchanged by History: America's Neglected Innovators.* New York: Putnam, 1979.

Richardson, Robert O. *The Weird and Wondrous World of Patents.* New York: Sterling Publishing, 1990.

Showell, Ellen and Amram, Fred M.B. *From Indian Corn to Outer Space: Women Invent in America.* Peterborough, N.H.: Cobblestone Publishing, 1995.

Sproule, Anna. *New Ideas in Industry: Women History Makers.* New York: Hampstead Press, 1988.

Vare, Ethlie Ann and Ptacek, Greg. *Women Inventors and Their Discoveries.* Minneapolis: The Oliver Press, 1993.

Veglahn, Nancy. *Women Scientists.* New York: Facts on File, 1991.

Weiss, Harvey. *How to be an Inventor.* New York: Thomas Y. Crowell, 1980.

Yenne, Bill. *100 Inventions That Shaped World History.* San Francisco: Bluewood Books, 1993.

You can read articles about women inventors in the June 1994 issue of *Cobblestone: The History Magazine for Young People.*

Places to Visit

**Inventure Place: National Inventors
  Hall of Fame**
221 S. Broadway
Akron, OH 44308

Anacostia Museum
1901 Fort Place S.E.
Washington, DC 20020

California Museum of Science and Industry
700 State Drive
Los Angeles, CA 90037

**Franklin Institute Science Museum and
  Planetarium**
20th and Benjamin Franklin Parkway
Philadelphia, PA 19103

Lawrence Hall of Science
University of California
Centennial Drive
Berkeley, CA 94720

Museum of Science
Science Park
Boston, MA 02114

Museum of Science and Industry
57th Street and Lake Shore Drive
Chicago, IL 60637

National Air and Space Museum
Sixth and Independence Avenue S.W.
Washington, DC 20560

National Museum of American History
24th Street and Constitution Avenue N.W.
Washington, DC 20560

Some Useful Addresses

Affiliated Inventors Foundation
2132 E. Bijou St.
Colorado Springs, CO 80909-5950

Invent America!
510 King St. Suite 420
Alexandria, VA 22314

Inventors Clubs of America
Box 450261
Atlanta, GA 30345

**Inventors Workshop International
  Education Foundation**
7332 Mason Ave.
Canoga Park, CA 91306

National Inventors Foundation
345 W. Cypress St.
Glendale, CA 91204

National Women's History Project
7738 Bell Road
Windsor, CA 95492

Society of Women Engineers
120 Wall St., 11th Floor
New York, NY 10005

The Women Inventors Project
1 Greensboro Drive, Suite 302
Etobicoke, Ontario M9W 1C8
Canada

A Summer Camp for Young Inventors

Hands-on activities in science, technology, and the arts are offered at Camp Invention, a weeklong summer camp held at various sites throughout the United States. The camps, sponsored by The National Inventors Hall of Fame, are for students in grades one through five. A companion program, Camp Ingenuity, was recently launched for students in grades six through eight. For information, call 1-800-968-4332.

Index

Albany, 30
Alden, John, 23
Annan, Charles, 15
antibiotics, 28-29
artificial breasts, 10-11
athlete's foot, 28

bacteria, 28-29
Barbie Doll, 8-11
breast cancer, 10-11
Brown, Dr. Rachel, 29-33

carpentry, 15
Chemical Pioneer Award,
   33
cultures, 27, 29-31
customs, 21-22

Edison, Thomas, 17

French Academy of
   Inventors, 23

fungi, 28-32

Handler, Barbie, 5-7
Handler, Elliot, 6
Handler, Ken, 6
Handler, Ruth, 5-11
Hazen, Dr. Elizabeth, 26-
   33

Ken Doll, 9
Kiddie Stool, 35
Knight, Margaret, 13-17

Low, Jeanie, 35
Mattel Company, 7-8
microorganisms, 26, 28, 32
Mycostatin, 32-33

New York City, 18-19, 21-
   22, 29-30
New York City Streets
   Commission, 19

New York State
  Department of Health, 27
nystatin, 32

paper bags, 13-16
paper dolls, 5
patents, 7, 14-17, 23, 32-
  33, 34-35
penicillin, 28
photography, 15, 23
pneumonia, 28

ringworm, 28
rotary engines, 17
Ruthton company, 11

silicone, 11
streptomycin, 29-30

textile mills, 14-15
trash carts, 20, 23
tuberculosis, 30

U.S. Patent Office, 15, 17,
  37
upholstery, 15

Washington, D.C., 15
Westover, Cynthia, 18-25
*Women's Ways of Earning
  Money*, 24

*Photo credits: Archives, Bristol-Meyers Squibb,
Princeton NJ: p. 33; Library of Congress
General Collections: p. 19; Library of
Congress Prints & Photo Division: pp. 20, 21,
23; Mattel Inc.: p. 4; US Patent & Trademark
Office: pp. 12, 24, 25, 36; Wadsworth Center,
Illustration Unit: pp. 27, 29.*